TIGERS ON THE
SILK ROAD

Other Books by the author:

The Eye's Circle (Rigmarole, Melbourne, 1974)
Tributaries of the Love-Song (Angus & Robertson,
      Pamphlet Series, Sydney, 1978)
Passengers to the City (Hale & Iremonger, Sydney, 1985)
Fish-Rings on Water (Forest Books, London, 1989)
Finding the Prince (Hearing Eye Pamphlet Series, London, 1993)
The Sleepwalker with Eyes of Clay (Forest Books, London, 1994)
Shifts (Hub Editions, Wisbech, Cambs., 1997)

TIGERS ON THE SILK ROAD

Katherine Gallagher

Arc
PUBLICATIONS
2000

Published by Arc Publications
Nanholme Mill, Shaw Wood Road
Todmorden, Lancs., OL14 6DA

Copyright © Katherine Gallagher 2000

Design by Tony Ward
Printed at the Arc & Throstle Press
Nanholme Mill, Todmorden, Lancs.

ISBN 1 900072 47 5

Acknowledgements:
Some of the poems in this collection appeared in
the pamphlet *Finding the Prince* (Hearing Eye, Lon-
don, 1993). *For Nizametdin Akhmetov* was pub-
lished under the title *Celebration* in *Sing Freedom!*
(Faber, 1991), and *Dancing* was included in the
Anthologies *As Girls Could Boast* (Oscars Press,
1994) and *Midday Horizon* (Round Table, Sydney,
1996). *The Ash Tree* was published in an Austral-
ian double-issue of *Poetry* (USA, 1996). *Jet Lag*
appeared in an Australian issue of *Poetry Review*
(UK, 1999). *Slippage* was published in an Austral-
ian issue of *Prism* (Canada, 2000).
Acknowledgements are also due to the Editors of
the following magazines and newspapaers: *The Age,
Earthwings, Hobo, Imago, Northern Perspective,
Quadrant, The Review, Salt, Southerly, Voices*
(Australia); *Acumen, Agenda, Envoi, The Interpret-
er's House, Lancaster Festival Anthology 1999,
London Magazine, Stand, Times Literary Supple-
ment, This Is, Writing Women* (UK); *Antipodes*
(US).

For Bernard and Julien

**The publishers acknowledge financial
assistance from Yorkshire Arts Board**

CONTENTS

Part I

You stick your tongue out cautiously
to get a taste of life:
snow or fire?
They burn the same.

Margareta Ekström,
translated from the Swedish by Eva Claeson

1969

I – Signs

There are the unseen dangers.
You expect my papers to blow all over Asia.
I note your frown, imagine myself lost,
a derelict with no forwarding address.

I'm all set, I say;
we've talked through this before.
You hover about me.
I'm wrapped – a parcel, ready.

There'll be shrines in Kathmandu,
the floating Taj Mahal, tigers maybe.
I'll ride a camel, visit Amritsar,
see Afghanistan's lapis-lazuli mountains
and explore the Silk Road to Istanbul.

I'll trail incense – jasmine, musk –
cardamon, saffron
streaming about my head:
feast on tandoori, korma, massala…

I won't be hungering
for love. But I'll expect
to eat your letters whole.

II – India

My bus crawls across India,
the afternoons catch me like sleep –
looking forward, looking back.
I pick through shelves of cloud,
see you everywhere – your face grinning
wryly, slipping through cirrus bands.

Inside the Vishnu shrine
I'm circling your head
homing on your words.
Through this thin-skinned paper,
(as I read, re-read them),
blurring, they mark my fingertips…

Listen to our voices,
yours still insistent
even as it's fading
faster, fast now…

III – Geneva

Though you're a hemisphere away
here you are: close-by –
our conjuring trick of never parting.

All the old stratagems of desire:
so much unfinished loving,
afternoons snatched out of the fire

as if we believed we could remake
what we had lived. That is love's lie.
With distance I have perfected it.

TRAVELLING LIGHT

I was a pair of eyes
travelling across Asia
the continent so big
only a little
to be covered each day.

All the giant Nikons
were in Vietnam
picking holes in a war
not far away.

My Minolta
managed a few
slide-souvenirs:

the bathers in the Ganges
among still-burning
funeral pyres;

the dull bronze tablets
along the Khyber pass
to honour British heroes;

the schoolchildren in Shiraz
who ran to our bus and said
Can you take our picture?

JUMPING IN

At fifteen,
finally glimpsing the sea –
its shorthand of cliffs
glistening in sun –

I headed
into waves shining behind
their fabulous white fringe
on the sea's shimmering pool.

Catching the white caps' coil, recoil
(like travellers, they came, they left),
I stayed, rocked in their silky
webbings, washed and washed by salt.

A boy taught me dog-paddle, crawl;
the blue salt helped me float.
Each day I swam out farther
seeking my own play of tides.

I remember a clutch of islands –
watched them, knew they would teach me
how to cling to waves.

In Memoriam for my Brother
for J.

A photograph slipped out of a bag –
I thought, I've got too many,
should edit them.
Then I saw it was you
sitting among rocks at Barbizon
in your blue pullover.

Behind us, Australia beckoned –
a grand water-lily
squat on the Pacific.
Would we ever make it here?

Those days, leaves scattering:
your skidding marriage;
my stalled affair.
We joked about beginnings.

A ladybird, burnt-scarlet,
blazed up your sleeve,
paused, turning back
on its path. You murmured *Hello*
and your eyes followed as it
flew off in dust-dry air.

PIPE DREAMS

Brand-new, half-hidden in tissue
fifteen pipes wait to be claimed.
I can't bear to give them away,
have had them twenty years –
Apple, Bulldog, Full bent,
meerschaum, porcelain, redwood,
expecting you to baptise them
in fire and ash:
blackstemmed
brier. Yours.

DANCING

Nothing has dulled my feel for earth,
its stern gravity-pull,
its cushion of dark.

Neighbours in the flat below
hear my feet tapping
while the rest of the house sleeps.
When I dance in daylight, boards creak:
samba, tango, waltz.

I have acres and acres to dance through,
recharging as I go. Sometimes I find a partner
in a shopping-mall or an uncut field,
my party-face sparking till I'm giddy.
I whirl through tiredness changing the beat,
everything spinning – I'm flying at last.

My eyes glisten, past bitterness –
I dance in my sleep.
Whole streets fly by me,
whole streets have started dancing.

JET LAG

I didn't go round the world. It went around me
crossing time zones in my sealed-off balloon,

following inflight-arrows across Europe,
Asia, Australia. Don't ask what day it is –

my body clock ticks in those concertinaed
intervals between borders and continents,

oceans urging them forward.
I can't find sleep. Instead I have birds

crisscrossing the lanes of my head.
They saw my airship slip by and me peering

through a window, setting my watch
by the stars. I'll catch up with this shaky life,

wrap it around me like a quick nap.
Leonardo put such problems on hold

with his *ornithopter*, needing wings
to flap before it could move.

So much for all that sky-gazing,
wanting to get off the ground.

Now I'll just sleep on possibilities.
I'm still thirty thousand feet up,

nudging clouds like a sunset, the day
slipping through my fingers.

NOMAD

That year you lost your husband
you wore one brave face after another.
Next thing, you kept changing countries.
Making a fresh start, you called it.

And still each new place sang,
claiming you against the dark.
He would have loved that –
you travelling solo pulled by both worlds.

His voice, breath – hand on your shoulder.
Arms and bodies linked on a bed
that moved like an ocean.
I wondered if you'd break.

Looking closer,
I saw you had broken –
you spent hours skeining days
that were all you had
to line your nomad shelter.

Part II

*What is the name for pockets of warmth
found even in deepest water?*

– Patricia Zontelli

THE SILENCE

The War's a long way off.
Among gum-trees on the Three-Chain
Road, I hear the buzz of cicadas,
carolling of magpies; wonder
who might come along.
A few Model T's, the latest Sedan?
All that silence, as if nothing's
happening under the sky.

A few possums and galahs
lie squashed on the road.
My sister Veronica's dead –
they say now she's an angel;
Jim Butler's missing in action.

Three months ago, on his first leave
Bradford Creek gave him
a Welcome-Home. He made
a speech in uniform, said the War
sent some people crazy.

At school, we have a newsbook
full of cuttings: Jim Butler's photo,
our side's progress through Sicily
and France; Pacific jungle-fights.

Now Jim Butler's a hero.
Soon he'll be
on the School Honour Roll
next to those from the Great War.

FROST COUNTRY

I
The kerosene-lamp flickers yellow.
Listening to the news over dinner
everyone talks at once. My mother's
voice, drumming through our childhoods,
interrupts, 'It's either you
or the wireless.' *Quiet*, before
the babble again. My father gallops
through stories – his childhood here,
the '14 drought, hand-feeding cattle,
putting the Ninety Acre in
for the first time, how
gold diggers turned farmers.

II
Outside, the evening's wide frost
is coming down. In the morning
the paddocks will be whiter
than snow. My fingers
will curl back with cold, beyond
their thrusts for information – sums,
copying my sister, half a column
behind. Later the teacher shows me
how to add up, take-away –
maths with fingers, counting.
Taking in a landscape, I'll soon find
my own way home from school.

III
Eastville – not even on the maps.
My uncle jokes it's the hub
of the universe, with a church
post office and school
set along the Three-Chain Road.
I make plans to paint
each parched acre green,
wave at the few cars that pass
as I walk the two miles
there and home.

1942

They'd hoped he'd be back for Christmas –
the lights shining down on him, the tree
somehow shielding off the horror. A break.
The family hadn't seen him as a soldier,
in his uniform, among harvested paddocks,
the dried stubble that pricked your legs.

Arriving home, he said *Merry Christmas*,
hugged people and slapped them on the back.
Wandered about the place, eyes crinkled
with strain, lines dug
into his forehead. So young, he seemed
to be either laughing or very sad
as though, in between,
there was nothing.

Bloodline

I – Horseman

Hat down over your eyes,
Snowy Mountains rider
straight from Killarney horse-and-gig men.
I revelled in the tales – the frantic reins,
whips in the air, horses panting,
your helter-skelter drives to Mass
along Eddington Road, gravel flying
racing your brothers, mad to be first.
If you balanced it later
with a fistfight, Dad –
well, here's looking at you
with your lad's face on.

Now years have stuck
to your skin. You've taken off
your *all-roads-lead-to*, know-how cloak.
Water's breaking over your head.
You're at the dam's edge:
the eldest son, your namesake,
teaches the rest of us to swim.
I hear the worry in your voice,
'I can't save you.'

Dad, you didn't try it.
You didn't even take your boots off
to paddle at the muddy rim.
I want you to jump in,
hold the water's curve,
the weight and shift of it.

II – The Electric Paddock

Three children mid-morning
    in a half-ploughed paddock
with a trusted Clydesdale
    and the dray,

picking up stones
    that block ploughshares
and hold up the team,
    helping their father.

Every few rounds he stops.
    The horses flick their tails
waiting in the pallid sun
    as he strides over,

with giant hands
    scoops up the iron-red stones;
in three minutes, picks up the same number
    that's taken us half the day.

We dawdle along: for once
    in the child's world we own
there's no hurry. He leaves us,
    promises a trip

to White Hills, Melbourne,
    the Big Smoke; the beach,
imagine, the sea; even the Zoo,
    a first for country kids.

We have time on our side,
    we'll do better on the stones,
even surprise him with the dray full
    before his next stop.

Soon we've lapsed
    back to dallying, noticing
the sky's lambswool rug changing shape,
    how some stones break into colours

when they smash: blue
    red, yellow, on the metal
of the dray; how the trees drop bark
    from their green canopies.

We stop to look at these eucalypts,
    wish for koalas,
know they won't be here. The magpies
    never stop singing, like blackbirds and thrushes

in school poems. I'm learning
    to love these gums: the brown-barked,
grey-barked – some dry, bare-limbed –
    the ring-barked.

III – Going to Mass in the '39 Pontiac

Pontiac: it sounded flash.
Elbows in and out,
we jostled aboard – on the same seat,
three wedged in front, two behind –
like potplants packed tight.
That Pontiac, secondhand,
housed five kids in the back.

There'd be my mother's sigh
as she smoothed her hair
after the rush between the last bath
and Dad's warning-roar
pacing us – *Five minutes to go!*
We'll be late... LATE!

He raced along the dirt roads
scattering dust; on his left,
Mother, one eye on him,
powdering her face Paris-pink;
a baby snugged between them.

IV – Burning Off

Warm autumn evening with a hint of frost.
He hands out rakes, forks, scrapes straw
into a pile and lights it. Starts us off,
pockets stuffed with paper, matches,
to make our own fires.

We love the burning, its pungent openness,
blink smoke in our eyes, turning the stubble
over and over, to set a fine red marge:
all this mapping.

We joke about hell, tall flames, pitchforks;
don't see ourselves as devils. There's no
dawdling, this evening's for burning –
for making new borders that crisscross
and disappear.
Dusk slides down
and our fires tail off.
              When we're done
the whole paddock's black:
black country
ready for the plough.

River Murray Reunion

I – Picnic

Mottle-barked, gigantic-trunked
red gums overhang
the water, drop shade –
mammoths with
the strength of oceans.

Nearby an old orchard
floats apple and pear blossom –
random confetti
waiting for a bride.

Today's a different celebration.
I hear the midday air
level into the buzz of flies
and a cicada drone. The thick tree-
silence is suddenly broken
by carillon peals from magpies,
Australia's nightingales,
reminding me I'm back.

For months I've imagined,
magnified the scene, peppered it
with anecdotes, have seized
the sky's still azure, felt
how the sun sweeps through me,
how my twin-lives have come
full circle to this...

Wind spikes the tablecloth
with sand, a speedboat skirrs
the river, briefly drowning
our voices and the secrets
not told in letters.

II – Verbatim

This is the bush,
I tell myself
looking for koalas and snakes,
echidnas, a kangaroo at least.
I imitate a kookaburra –
(my party act for foreigners).
The children cheer.

We wait for the kookaburras
to answer –
one long scarf of laughs.
That's supposed to warn
of interlopers.
I smile – an interloper,
but with my best face on.

FREE

That afternoon, you talked so much
telling us about your holiday beau,
a widower with the blarney touch.

You said it was just a mild fling
with lots of laughs and ravenous chat –
a little adventure on the wing.

And your seventy-five years shook,
ironing out their creases;
you swore you wouldn't have to look

further for someone perfect to love
and be loved by, your voice almost shy.
        But nothing, you said, could move

you to remarry – it was too late
for that, to start over.
And he, true as true, said he'd wait

though you insisted you'd live alone –
after all these years, only
wanting a life of your own.

I didn't want to go into the house –
knew I'd find you somewhere
in the garden, your *botanicus flora*
favourite place. I could scarcely bear
to see the tidiness, everything just so –
spade and rake against the wall
as if you'd been working here all morning
among rowans, lavender, wattles,
azaleas, and the weeping cherry
you'd planted yourself.

I knew you'd be impatient to hear
what was in flower: the clumps of hyacinths
around the cannas, irises, daffodils,
your delphinium patch. *Plant and weed*
you taught me the names: japonica,
plumbago, buttercup, nettle…

When I took some cherry blossom
to the hospital, your face lit up.
We talked about the Spring
Horticultural Show (your project);
our chat brittled into details
of your latest tests – more to come.
You touched the pink
petals, turned your head away,
'When that prunus is out,
I'm always home.'

MY MOTHER'S GARDEN
i.m. C.G.

Banksias, lemon gums, golden wattle: fire-prone
native trees she was afraid of planting close
to the house. And she preferred the softer greens
of the Europeans. Long summer evenings she'd walk
among the fragrances – lavender, jasmine, rose.
Leaning into the plants, talking to them,
pulling off dried leaves, dead-heading blooms.
Another snip? More water?
She'd scoop up canna lilies, dahlias, daisies
that cascaded over her freckled, weatherworn arms.
She saw herself forever in her *Park*.

Now I circle the rowans, golden ash,
flowering cherry; follow lines of lavender
and bougainvillea – exploding purple.
My feet don't tire of this walk
I've come back to for her sake and mine.

The current owners of the house left the gate open –
they may come back, tell me to go. I have my alibi,
talk to my mother through the soles of my feet.

Part III

The tiny clusters of whitebeard heath are in flower.
Their scent has drawn to them moths from how far away?

– Judith Wright

The Gondola at Santa Maria Miracoli, Venice

Take a marriage on water, with gondolier-
boatmen, dressed in white and red satin,
the artefacts of *ricchezze* – it's already
a grand occasion – the boatmen expect
to row the couple to their tower and not turn back.
It's natural for the wedding-party
to be enveloped by its own *bonomia*, gravitas:
family, friends, the priest's words singing the air.

A vista of marble and roses, *felicità*
candles sweeping the darkness, and guests' faces
illumined as they stand for the couple,
about to pass this first test of their lives together –
to board the gondola on lapping water,
the calm-boat lined with velvet and gardenias:
the sound of churchbells crashing behind them
and the tower, its fiery vane, always ahead.

TATTOO-SPEAK

Friends on one wrist
Be on the other –
with each hand-flick
he floats his message
to lovers, all-comers,
the green-eyed public,
bit players
everywhere

(who may wonder
at the ease of it:
his map of two words,
their crimson zigzags
against each turquoise sea)

moving at their own pace
past the glare of his map –
two words with
a long-time glow,
his spur-of-the-moment
lines on skin's parchment,
guarding a riddle
writ small writ large.

POEM FOR A SHALLOT

I am fooled.
You insist on the secret of skins –
how perfectly each wraps you.

You compartmentalize,
I don't know how.
I can peel you back to nothing.

I hunt for what isn't there –
layer upon layer –
down to your cagey heart.

When I try to get away
you've snuck into my breath, eyes,
making me cry

into my hands.

NEVER ENOUGH

We throw kisses
sky-high, round
the surface of the planet,
leave them
on the ground
to cushion our feet.

I kiss your breath away.
You tease me down
the mountain,
kiss me hollow, stave
my hunger.

When I lose you
I find you
with kisses.
We are careless,
have covered fields
with them, come
full circle.

PREDATORS

They know how to wait,
circling his head
like a crown of thorns
on invisible wire.

When I swish
they hang still,
don't budge. My son
clings to me and laughs.

He's never seen such
fat-bellied mosquitoes,
thinks it's a game
like the time
I scooped him back
from a child snatcher.

April Summer Fever

The south of England
has undressed
for the day, the beach spangled
end to end: a crowdswell
edging closer to the coast
and the hazy landface
opposite.

Slim bodies arching,
our children skim stones –
watch a speedboat scuff
the mesmerising flatness:
back to their game –
throw, splash, throw, splash, throw
against the waves' diamanté glare.
It's like a film-set
(endless retakes, getting it right):
Watch, watch, they insist
trying to throw further each time.

RECKONING

Each foot taking us
faster-slow, shadows
before the range
we angled towards it.
Beyond the scattered
settlements, our paths
spanned out.

Soon we hiked by
waterfalls;
our tracks zigzagged
the mountain's furred skin.
This was like work:
the weight and sweat
of the climb
pulling us back
in our push towards
that line
far away enough
to meet the sky.

Stepping over bramble
we urged each other forward,
leaving everything we knew
behind. The mountain
owned us. Our faces
wore together
like two sides of a coin.

Part IV

What is to come sleeps in the bud
now tilting upwards towards a thinning light.

– Colette Inez

THE ASH TREE

The woodman has the tree in his grip.
He talks to its heart: thirty per cent
of the crown must be cut – it will be denser,
go into itself, discover new shoots.

Surgeon, he sits back in the rope-saddle;
ear protectors shield him from the saw's rasp.
Slowly the limbs are looped, excised.

No breeze, nothing disturbs the leaves
but this interloper intent on his task.
Linking himself to the tree,
swinging on up, making notches.

He goes for the highest branches,
pulls ropes tighter, skids about.
The tree is being bargained with.

This is a listed tree. Fifty years back,
it survived fire – scars blacken the trunk.

Today it lays a lean shadow over the lawn.
History crowds in – we cannot see
the heartwood, sapwood, the rings
carrying each year to the outer bark...

The woodman is coming to terms
with the tree. It will outlive him.

THIRTEEN

Smooth in my palm,
it glows like polished cedar;
on the other side – the dull map
of a monk's tonsure:
the first conker.
I always find it for him.

This time he leaves it,
Come on, Mum,
it's only the seed
of a chestnut...

I pick it up, rub it shiny
in my pocket.
There's a tree inside.

KNEBWORTH PARK

A cave of air softens,
hovers over our heads.
We've waited all year for this:
the March lull, the park
almost tourist-free.

Put your ear
to this unsaddled soil,
sound out the mating-calls
of otters, rabbits, voles;
hear horses' hoofbeats
pound nearer-far.

I have made an altar of calm
among these ageing oaks,
lines of stiff-backed trees.

Our walk circles the ancient house,
grounds set off by daffodils.
A five-year-old sings a nursery rhyme,
wanting to pat sheep. Their beady eyes
distract, promising only puzzles.

We call ourselves comfortable explorers,
notice a wine-glass left among the ferns.
A squirrel skids into wintry hiding.
As the light fades, we study
each other's faces
for signs of sun.

A Visit to the War Memorial, Canberra

We have scratched their names
on the national bronze

cradled them
in a dark photograph

We have collected their medals
ranked them behind glass

carried their relics
through mirages and warnings

We have taken their legends
the words that couldn't halt

the backdrop-massacres
and tainted forests

We have heard dry laughter
breaking their silences

as they kept marching
despite their chagrin

bagging their history
in the tally of requiems

whispering their names
over and over

in halls of recognition
where feet crunch on boards

and conversations
breed silences

Say that the word is *gall:*
cusped, broken on the tongue:
redolent of battles that appal.
Say that the word is *gall.*
Heroes, ordinary blokes, all
sung for Sari Bair, dying young.
Say that the word is *gall* –
cusped, broken on the tongue.

LES ÉTANGS DE LA SOMME

Icy trees fringe ponds.
A man in a boat, fishing.

The sky clears its white light, unhooks
the radiance of clouds, muslin over blue.

Birds' nests hug branches –
fish-bone trees.

A crow releases its iron caws.
Then silence. The sky blurs

gives nothing away.
It has monuments of air.

We pass, itinerants
on no particular pilgrimage,

led back to flimsy mornings
when they say birdsong

was the last thing soldiers heard
before going *over the top*.

SLIPPAGE

I
They have found an answer,
those people talking to their plants.

Tongues rising,
breath following breath.

Through a carbon dioxide veil
plants take in exhalations.

II
In new council-flat blocks,
the windows are uniformly small,

rationing the view. It was never
like this on the mountain.

Years of looking at guidebooks,
wanting to camp in the hills.

III
There was no deluge, only equators
that saw the rivers spill over.

The sky might boil, we would
cover our heads, remembering

love, where we had delayed it —
this fate of avoidance.

We wear out hearts on old sleeves,
tamed by the usual risks.

There is still the wash of sun —
another day, the drying summer.

JANUARY, 1994
(after a news item on Sarajevo – January 23, 1994)

Between the face and the hand
there has been a reckoning

Between the gut and the eye
there has been an accident

Between the heart and the field
there has been a hunger

Between the arm and the gun
there has been a killing

And the deaths wrap themselves
in newsprint and celluloid

with snipers and firebrands
mortars and silences

In the name of the cross,
a sign, an echo

In the rush of a cloud,
a storm, a fissure

In the crack of a bird's egg,
a watching, an evolution

In the smudge of a promise,
a wish, a warning

*

Don't let your children out to play
not even in the middle of the day

*

Alipasno Polje is a crowded suburb,
there'd been several falls of snow;
the mothers watched at windows,
heard the children's pleas to go.

One hundred left the tower blocks
wanting to be out in the air;
their mothers waved and waited,
and begged them to take care.

The cameras come in easy,
the cameras come in fast –
the cameras watched like spies
as the children scrambled past.

They rolled around on the ground,
pitched snowballs and skidded about
like any children suddenly
free just to race and shout.

It had been quiet in Alipasno Polje,
quiet for a couple of days.
Of little military value, it was
kept under enemy-gaze.

The first shell fell quite short,
the second came in close;
the third fell outside the tower blocks
and a zigzag of terror rose.

One child lost an arm and a leg,
one had his head blown away
playing there in the first white snow
on a sky blue winter's day.

FOR NIZAMETDIN AKHMETOV

'You don't know how I longed for this...' – N.A.

Freedom, forgiveness... the words
repeat themselves, carried through
the audience like kindling
catching fast. A prisoner at nineteen,
twenty years on, he's a man uncurling
his tongue: *love, forgiveness,*
the words again, his gift, as they
collect, fly from the rostrum.

Earlier, he shipped out words
hidden in logs: his poems
that would not lie down,
that have become his passport.
He tells of weeks in asylums
(legs swollen from beatings) –
wondering if they'd be amputated.

No one here can reach him.
He is a man seeing spring
differently. He thanks his liberators,
praises newness. Daffodils
through the window
outline him in gold.

TJINDERALLY ODYSSEY
for Eva Johnson

Aboriginal women
close about,

keening tribal songs
shuffling hours, histories

the rough muslin of days
carried in suitcases:

journeys, whispers,
that time in the mission

after they were taken away
to be 'educated',

searching for family
mothering each other –

some at last finding
their own mothers

inching back
to the land, a foothold,

bit by bit,
humbly

angrily
plaiting their stories.

The Lines on her Palm

I've burnt the barn –
an accident, my fault:
my plans awry,
so what?

I'm the farm hand
who talked to herself,
piled up grain
and worked like a man.

The job was never easy
but I liked that feeling
of giving all I had –
my inheritance.

I slept one eye open
on my few possessions:
the canvas suitcase,
my mother's glass bracelet.

What bargains I drove
lumping corn over
that barn's rickety floor!

I swore I'd make
my fortune, head out
the perimeter-gate
to an uncharted terrain.

The wind blows ashes
around me. They settle,
cover the soil.
I see my losses.

Stand up, try to keep
feet steady;
stalk beneath
the sky's shreds.

IN HER SHOES

The silvery-white scales come in –
announce themselves, mean stayers.
She ghosts out, trying coal tars,
ultraviolet, baths – anything for a cure.
The sun wears through each sore.

No part of her escapes; she tries
to hide as red plaques
colonise arms, shoulders,
trunk, scalp, calamined.

We fight the wars of envy. I imagine
she'd like to peel off my smooth skin,
do an exchange in the usual way of sisters
wearing each other's sweaters, track suits.
I hear her ask again, *Why me?*

Steroids, Vitamin D cream –
*I've tried so many miracle
remedies, I should have been cured
by now... A new skin, a new me?*

I remember a day before all this
when beach sun fell on
her bare shoulders, soft as air.

HUNGER

She is thinking of the last time he touched her –
how he stroked her, said she was losing weight

as if it represented a country they had to get to, as if
the fat could curl back to the bone like years undone.

And she saw they stood between their shadows and the wolf
who howls for them in the night.

MEETING THE OZONE LAYER
for Giorgio de Chirico

You take headless people
into a new dimension,
making a lateral-spun
sharp order: each pencilled-in brain
born in colour, and shading
like a love affair that's always
changing. How many charcoal
shades can there be?
It's not a colour
I could love: gun-metal,
the war-clouds
in a wraparound skirt.

You keep leaving the cities –
their arcades, buildings, urgent
with matchbox lives beating the wars
(undertones: a train that
can't stop.) Mannequins stare
at humans feigning sleep
on the edge of parks or gardenless
towers. Set up a mirror.
What if imaginations crackle
with a worn-out scent,
the masks brimming over?
Wanting the end
of the end of desire, dreading
the grey armour we are given.

The war of colours may be
the last. It is as if all is well:
the opera starting, the house filling,
your heart settling sooner
than you know. Look, the people
with their heads in place
are listening harder and harder,
metamorphosing through winters,
continents. Behind rainbow-
coloured curtains, the owls sleep
in daylight as though normal,
the mirrors are turned outwards.

Part V

...rock salt...
a cathedral through which light passes,
crystal of the sea, abandoned
by the waves

(Pablo Neruda, trans. by Robert Bly)

POINSETTIAS
for M.

I
Daily she chides
her mirror:

who is this woman
staring back

turning the glass around,
twisting its magnifier

seeing a lifetime's portraits
paraded like miniatures –

herself at fifteen in the school-
concert, on her wedding-day,

in the Alexandra Chorus,
at her son's graduation?

She gathers in her few strands
under the blonde-curled wig

studies her pinched skin,
wanting a sign,

a rouge
in her cheeks

an opposite of surrender.
The love of red will save her.

*

Solo lamps articulate
each starred bush. Leaves become flowers,
flowers become leaves,
fine red stems shedding fire, sunrise-bright.

She sees herself walking through
their thick wall, a cascade of scarlet
at the hospital entrance.

Daily the tread through white-lined leaves,
the bloodless veined maps, red-topped –
their blazes reminders.

When she grows tired, it is right
to look away, forget
the furrowed richness.

Three months have scarred me...
She studies photographs
from last Christmas:

she and her sons
among the prized
dye-bright coal-flowers

that will not be extinguished,
will fall off the stem
and fold in at their own pace.

                    *

Her visitors trailed messages of fire.
She touched the poinsettias –
velvet-strong petals, easily bruised.
If only some of their fire could stay for her,
help her sleep. One operation after another.
She followed her charts; read *'Terminal'*
(the doctors' notes carelessly
left on her bed) as if she were
strong enough to know the worst –
the tumour's shifts and moods,
as though her body had stopped
in its tracks, to remind her of the
recklessness of cells speeding up.
The word *'Terminal'* hammered her.
If only she hadn't read it...

                    *

The poinsettias stopped flowering,
their fire finally dissolved in air.
She cut the stems back to half their length,
fed them every fortnight
when the new growth began.
Without their red, the painted leaves,
she felt displaced, settled
into a green of hesitations,
willing herself to obey the plants:
Don't overfeed, use tepid water…

She would carry them
or leave a message for her sons
to bring them from the cellar
next Christmas, nearly
a year away now.

                    *

The call of plants: the yew
making Taxol that enters her veins
with a slow drip, drip,
taking her through the nexus
of these days – the means, as if
health were a luxury, declaring itself
time after time, the Taxol
winding into her cells,
plumping them back to life.

Again, the treatment – *like
flu and a torrid hangover*
– Taxol, an experiment,
her latest miracle-cure
in the wings. If this doesn't work,
they'll try another.
Tamoxifen. Trials, the wait.
Always the play with percentages
and carcinomas haunting
the space that's left to her.

She wills herself well, meditates,
tells her healer and the others
who offer remedies –
teas, leaves, honey –
It is *mind over matter*...
They're testing another drug –
Will these cures be ready in time?
she whispers, thinking of next
Christmas, her children –
the body that made them
betraying her.

II
I bring her vegetables,
wholegrain flour and eggs.

She jokes about
eating for her tumour.
I can't bear
to hear her say
she's begun to know it.

She pats her swollen stomach,
face twisting in a smile –
I have come this far.

More plans: memory boxes
for her sons; her husband
with such hopes
for them, his paintings –
already dead.

Her face, gritty hard.
*I can allow myself
only so much grief...*

                    *

We listen to the *Kyrie*
from Bach's Mass in D.

She tells me
it's her favourite
and the *tour-de-force*
for her next concert.

She turns up the volume –
I have to sing it
no matter what…

She hums an aria,
asks me to sing
soprano to her alto.

How can I enter the mood
that carries her along?

Singing makes me tired
but frees me –
her voice lifts

flying; drops,
tugged by a weight;
lifts again;
wavering…

*

Across the street
the florist is putting out
cyclamens, irises, hot-house
daffodils flown in.

Christmas is three months
away. *It'll soon be time*
for my poinsettias…

I think of how their wildfire
catches, spreading
around her.

She says she must
have them ready,
flowering on time.

We read her diary, make plans –
a trip to Kew Gardens
if she is well enough.

*You know those doctors' notes,
I never should have read them...*

She offers me bread,
makes several loaves
to give away.

*Nothing's important any more
but this*, she says, playing
her own game against
all odds,

letting the bread's
thiamine and riboflavin
keep her veins.

Under deft fingers:
curves of dough.
Each loaf is cooling
to its own shape.

KATHERINE GALLAGHER was born in 1935 in Maldon, Victoria, graduated from the University of Melbourne in 1963 and taught in Melbourne for five years before moving to Europe, living first in London and then in Paris for nine years. In 1979 she moved back to London, working as a secondary teacher and, after 1990, as a poetry tutor for the Open College of the Arts, Jacksons Lane, and Barnet College, London. During this time she has been co-editing *Poetry London*, as well as working extensively with primary school children. In 1978, she was awarded a Writer's Fellowship from the Literature Board, Australia Council, and in 1981, she won the Brisbane Warana Poetry Prize. Her book *Passengers to the City* (Hale & Iremonger, Sydney, 1985) was shortlisted for the Australian National Poetry Award.

Tigers on the Silk Road is her third full-length collection and follows her translation of Jean-Jacques Celly's *Le Somnambule aux Yeux d'Argile* (*The Sleepwalker with Eyes of Clay*, Forest Books, 1994). She also writes children's poetry and many of her children's poems have appeared in anthologies.